PREPPER SUPPLIES CHECKLIST

A Simple Guide to Emergency Preparedness

BY: NETTIE DAVID
www.PreppersSurvive.com

Contributors: photos: Nettie David, prepper calendar photos: Canva.com, cover design: https://www.fiverr.com/vikiana, illustrations: https://www.fiverr.com/nikitagarets

CONTENTS

1   Introduction 3

2   Prepper Supplies Checklist 4

   2.1   Prepper Supplies Mile-Markers 4

   2.2   Water Checklist 7

   2.3   Food Checklist 8

      2.3.1   Meal Plan 10

      2.3.2   Kitchen Checklist 11

   2.4   Warmth & Light Checklist 12

      2.4.1   Power Outage Kit 13

      2.4.2   Off-Grid Room 14

      2.4.3   Energy & Fuel Checklist 15

   2.5   First Aid Kit Checklist 17

   2.6   Hygiene Supplies Checklist 19

   2.7   Communication Checklist 21

   2.8   Emergency Contact List 22

   2.9   Family Identification 23

   2.10 Protection & Hunting Checklist 25

   2.11 Financial Checklist 26

   2.12 Bugout Bag Checklist 28

3   How to Use the Prepper Calendar 30

4   Prepper Calendar 31

5   Extra Checklist 32

6   Thank You 38

1 INTRODUCTION

About the Author:

I learned the importance of saving money and stashing resources for hard times, at an early age. My father had a seasonal job at a cannery which meant that he was laid-off a couple of months each year. Food storage was necessary for my family because we relied on it to get us through the winter until the working season started again. As my parents worked hard to provide for our family of ten, they taught me the importance of planning, ingenuity, resourcefulness, and self-reliance.

I was married in 2001, the beginning of what economists now refer to as "the lost decade." During that ten years, the stock market had some ups and downs but ultimately ended where it began. It was also the beginning of the "war on terrorism" which was brought about by the tragic events of September 11th. In 2008, my husband and I both worked in real estate when the real estate market crashed and ushered in the period known as "the great recession."

These and many other experiences throughout my life have taught me the value of emergency preparedness. My husband and I have survived economic crisis and cyclical markets with an astonishing level of comfort because of these preparedness principles. None of us know for sure what the next stage of our life will bring. My experience has taught me that comfort and peace of mind are more readily available to the individuals and family who prepare for hard times as well as prosperity. It is easy to get overwhelmed because there is so much to do. Prepping is not a sprint (or even a marathon) it is a continuous journey. There is a peace that comes from having a written plan, setting attainable goals, and working towards those goals.

About this Book:

This book began as a blog. It is a compilation of several articles and checklists you will find throughout prepperssurvive.com. Over the years, I have had many requests to create a book from Preppers Survive blog articles. This book was created to meet that request. The following pages are in a workbook format. It is designed for the users to develop an emergency preparedness plan specific to their families. Each section can help you evaluate the supplies you currently have available, the location of supplies, provide ideas on items you may potentially lack, and checklists to measure progress toward your preparedness goals.

How to use this book:

1. Read the supply ideas in each section (starts on page 7).

2. Write in your top three off-grid choices in the side column.

3. Write in the additional supplies you have and want in the checklist graph. If you need more space or an additional category, a larger checklist is provided on pages 32 & 37.

4. Check off the items you already have.

2 PREPPER SUPPLIES CHECKLIST

While vacationing in Kauai, there was a storm warning. I called down to the hotel's front desk to find out where they would evacuate the guests if a hurricane hit. Next, I evaluated the supplies I would take with me. Rather than weighing the value of each item in my suitcase, I have found that it is much faster to think about the categories of preparedness and pack accordingly.

There is no way to predict how much notice you will receive before disaster strikes. I have read accounts of warning-times of 13 minutes for tornados, 15 minutes for wildfires, and 20 minutes for tsunamis. People panic when they are forced to make a quick decision about what to take and often will grab impractical items that are in their line of sight before hurrying out the door. Having a plan can help you move from the frozen state of "what do I do?" to an actionable preparedness mindset. The prepper categories that I use as a guide to quickly gather supplies are water, food, warmth, light, first-aid, hygiene, communication, protection, and financial.

Next time you find yourself away from home, think about your new environment and how quickly you could bug out with supplies if a disaster had just been announced. Mentally run through the nine preparedness categories and evaluate items nearby that would be useful to take with you in a quick evacuation scenario.

Prepper Supplies Mile-Markers

Goal Reached:	4 days - bug out kit	2 weeks	1 month	6 months	1 year	2 years	Self-reliant
Water	○	○	○	○	○	○	○
Food	○	○	○	○	○	○	○
Warmth	○	○	○	○	○	○	○
Light	○	○	○	○	○	○	○
First aid	○	○	○	○	○	○	○
Hygiene	○	○	○	○	○	○	○
Protection	○	○	○	○	○	○	○
Communication	○	○	○	○	○	○	○
Financial	○	○	○	○	○	○	○

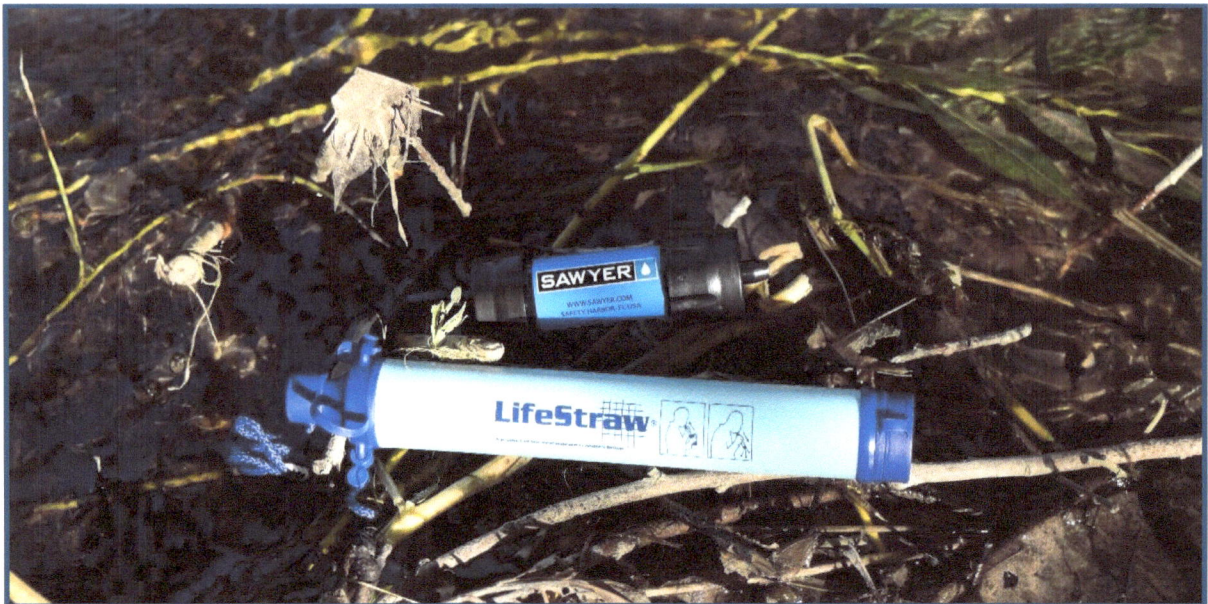

A person can only survive about three days without water, that is why it is first on the priority list. FEMA suggests having (1) gallon of water per person per day for drinking, cooking, rehydrating, and cleaning. If you are storing water for more than one person, the gallons can quickly add up.

Storing drinking water long term takes planning and prep work.

1. Start by calculating how much water you want to store for your household. Write down the total number of household members then multiply that number by how many days of water reserves you want. If I had a family of five and wanted 14 days of water reserves, then I should store 70 gallons of water.

2. Decide what water storage containers work best for your family. Label each one with the month and year when it is filled with water. To keep your drinking water fresh and free from contaminants the water containers need to be emptied and refilled regularly.

3. Add water filters to your emergency preparedness supplies. Make sure the water filters remove contaminants such as bacteria and parasites.

4. Locate the nearest body of water in your community. Use an online map service or purchase a city map, if you need help locating the nearest body of water. Sometimes you can pick-up a free local map from your city's Parks and Recreation Department or at the library. Walk the route from your house to the nearest body of water once you have a route plotted.

How many gallons of water storage do you currently have?

Item	x	How Many You Have	Equals	Total Gallons
5-gallon water jug	x		=	
1- gal. juice containers refilled with water	x		=	
3- gal. case of water bottles	x		=	
	x		=	
	x		=	
	x		=	
	x		=	
Total Gallons of Water Storage				

What is your Water Storage Goal?

How many people live in your household? 1._____

How many days of water reserves do you want? 2._____

Multiply lines 1 and 2 (gallons you will need) 3._____

How many gallons of water do you currently have? 4._____

Subtract line 3 & line 4 (total gallons still needed) _____

2.1 WATER FILTERS/PURIFIERS *List your survival filtering resources*	How many gallons does it filter?
○	
Circle what the filter removes: *Bacteria, Protozoa, Viruses, Heavy Metals, Chemicals*	
○	
Circle what the filter removes: *Bacteria, Protozoa, Viruses, Heavy Metals, Chemicals*	
○	
Circle what the filter removes: *Bacteria, Protozoa, Viruses, Heavy Metals, Chemicals*	

Off-grid resources are helpful in a power outage. I believe in having 3 off-grid methods in each category.

For example, boiling water may not be a practical way to purify water in every emergency situation. Boiling water takes several minutes to lessen the threats of harmful bacteria, viruses, and parasites. When water is boiled, it causes a portion of it to evaporate so if water is scarce or it's a scorching hot day a microfilter waterstraw may be more practical.

Purifying water ideas:

Bleach, boil, micro filter straws, purification tablets, carbon filtration system, ultraviolet purifier, solar disinfection. Keep in mind expiration dates and the amount of water each process can purify.

Water supply ideas:

Bathtub liners, canteen, containers for collecting water, rain gutter catchers, water storage containers, 32-ounce water bottles, water bladder, water siphon.

2.2 FOOD CHECKLIST

Grains:

30 lbs of grain per person per month. Total family members _____ x 30 = _____ x by _____ months supply = _____lbs

Grain ideas: wheat, white flour, corn meal, rice, pasta, oats, pancake mix, buckwheat

Food Item	#lbs You Have	Location	#lbs You Need
_____	_____	_____	_____
_____	_____	_____	_____
_____	_____	_____	_____
_____	_____	_____	_____
_____	_____	_____	_____
_____	_____	_____	_____
_____	_____	_____	_____
Total:	_____		_____

Beans & Legumes:

10 lbs of beans per person per month. Total family members _____ x 10 = _____ x by _____ months supply = _____lbs

Beans ideas: black beans, pinto, refried, kidney, garbanzo, navy, red, lentils, split pea

_____	_____	_____	_____
_____	_____	_____	_____
_____	_____	_____	_____
_____	_____	_____	_____
_____	_____	_____	_____
_____	_____	_____	_____
Total:	_____		_____

Dairy Products:

2 lbs of dairy per person per month. Total family members _____ x 2 = _____ x by _____ months supply = _____lbs

Dairy ideas: cheese, milk (powdered, condensed, evaporated or milk substitute)

_____	_____	_____	_____
_____	_____	_____	_____
_____	_____	_____	_____
Total:	_____		_____

Salt:

1 lb of salt per person per month. Total family members _____ x 1 = _____ x by _____ months supply = _____lbs

Salt	_____	_____	_____

Meats / Meat Substitutes:

120 servings of meat per person per mo. Family members ____ x 120 =_____ x by ____ months supply =_____

Meat ideas: beef, chicken, pork, dry eggs, tuna, jerky (Canned, dehydrated, freeze dried, frozen)

_____ _____ _____ _____
_____ _____ _____ _____
_____ _____ _____ _____
_____ _____ _____ _____
_____ _____ _____ _____

Total: _____ _____

Fats & Oils:

2 lbs of fats & oils per person per month. Total family members ____ x 2 =_____ x by ____ mo. supply =___lbs

Fats & oil ideas: peanut butter, cooking oil, butter, mayo, salad dressing, nuts

_____ _____ _____ _____
_____ _____ _____ _____
_____ _____ _____ _____

Total: _____ _____

Sugars:

5 lbs of sugars per person per month. Total family members ____ x 5 =_____ x by ____ months supply =_____lbs

Sugar ideas: granulated sugar, brown sugar, honey, molasses, jellies, fruit, drink mix

_____ _____ _____ _____
_____ _____ _____ _____
_____ _____ _____ _____
_____ _____ _____ _____

Total: _____ _____

Vegetables, Herbs, Spices:

120 servings of veggies per person per mo. Family members ____ x 120 =_____ x by ____ months supply =_____

Vegetable ideas: corn, green beans, tomatoes, potato flakes, dehydrated onions

_____ _____ _____ _____
_____ _____ _____ _____
_____ _____ _____ _____
_____ _____ _____ _____
_____ _____ _____ _____

Total: _____ _____

2.2.1 Meal Plan

When developing your food storage goals, it is important to have a two-week meal plan and the recipes for each meal printed out. The recipes you choose should be meals your family will eat using food storage ingredients.

Meal ideas for the calendar below:

Breakfast: Pancakes, Oatmeal, Granola, Buckwheat

Lunch: Soups, Stews, Chili, Bean Salads

Dinner: Spaghetti, Tuna Casseroles, Fried Rice & Veggies

For recipes & meal ideas visit: http://www.prepperssurvive.com/food-storage-cookbooks-pdf/

	SUN	MON	TUES	WED	THURS	FRI	SAT
Breakfast							
Lunch							
Dinner							
Breakfast							
Lunch							
Dinner							

2.2.2 Kitchen Checklist

Kitchen Tools	Location
○ Baby food grinder (hand crank)	
○ Cast iron cookware	
○ Can Opener	
○ Cooking utensils (stainless steel)	
○ Mortar & pestle	
○ Meat grinder (hand crank)	
○ Pot holders (leather)	
○ Pressure cooker	
○ Oil press (hand crank)	
○ Thermometers (no batteries)	
○ Wheat grinder (hand crank)	
○	
○	
○	
○	
○	

Kitchen Supplies	Location
○ Baking pans (disposable)	
○ Dish soap	
○ Disinfecting wipes	
○ Garbage bags	
○ Plates, bowls, & cups (disposable)	
○ Scrubbers	
○ Tinfoil & plastic wrap	
○ Utensils (disposable)	
○	
○	
○	
○	

Having off-grid options are helpful in a power outage. Below list 3 off-grid methods you want in your emergency supplies:

Cooking

○ 1st _____

○ 2nd _____

○ 3rd _____

Cooking ideas: grill, solar oven, dutch oven, camping stove (wood burning & propane).

Food Preservation

○ 1st _____

○ 2nd _____

○ 3rd _____

Food preservation ideas: canning, fermentation, ice box, freeze dried, root cellar, dehydrate.

Warmth & Light

Having off-grid options are helpful in a power outage. Below list 3 off-grid methods you could use in your emergency supplies:

Warmth

○ 1st _____

○ 2nd _____

○ 3rd _____

Warmth ideas: *fireplace, propane heater, solar windows, blankets (wool, jean, down), winter clothes, snow clothes, a heavily insulated room.*

Light

○ 1st _____

○ 2nd _____

○ 3rd _____

Lighting ideas: *kerosene lamp, candle, flashlight, solar light, crank lantern.*

2.3 WARMTH & LIGHT CHECKLIST	Location its stored
○	
○	
○	
○	
○	
○	
○	
○	
○	
○	
○	
○	
○	

Staying warm is vital for good health and survival. There are several ways to provide warmth. The checklist above is determined off of the three options you list on the left side of this page. For example, if you choose a fireplace for your heat source then write in the checklist above: ax, chainsaw, splitter, matches, etc.

Light plays an important role in our emotional well-being. When there's no light our minds can get overly active, and in a crisis, darkness can feed our fears. Lights allow us to prepare meals, read, work, and feel safe when the sun goes down. Some Hurricane Sandy victims were without power for 13 days. Hurricane Katrina victims were without power for 23 days (http://bigstory.ap.org/article/power-outage-time-after-sandy-not-extraordinary).

2.3.1 Power Outage Kit

Power outages happen. Some storms or accidents disable neighborhood power for weeks. How comfortable would you be if there was no city power available for two weeks? Every home should have a power outage kit. You will want to consider the main prepper essentials when assembling a power outage kit for yourself or your family: water, food, warmth, light, first aid, hygiene, and communication. The picture above is a picture of my power outage kit (water, food, first aid & hygiene are stored separately).

Power Outage Kit

❍ *Indoor Safe Propane Heater*

❍ *Solar Lanterns*

❍ *NOAA Radio & Flashlight (hand crank)*

❍ *Battery Bank Cell Phone Charger*

❍ *Propane Cooking Stove*

❍ *Batteries*

❍ *Matches*

2.3.2 Off-Grid Room

Have you ever considered which room in your home would make the best Off-Grid Room in an emergency? After reading Fernando Aguirre's book, The Modern Survival Manual: Surviving the Economic Collapse, I began looking at my living space with a new perspective. The book is based on the author's experience living through the 2001 economic collapse of Argentina. Fernando describes in detail how his family all slept in the same room to keep warm when they lost power.

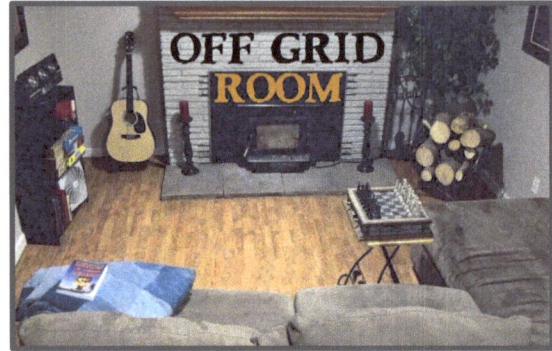

To have an Off-Grid Room you do not need costly, complicated solar panels or a bug-out location in the mountains. Create an Off-Grid Room by designating an ordinary room in your home to be the gathering place in a power outage.

Choose a room that will conserve your emergency resources.

Think about it, if you have multiple people in your home and everyone wants emergency lights in each room that can use up resources fast. If you have an emergency heater, are you going to use it in the draftiest part of your home? Below are ideas that will help you choose a room in your home that will help you maximize the emergency resources you have available.

Room Specifications:

- Small – most portable off grid heaters can heat an area between 200 and 600 sqft, depending on the heater. The smaller the room, the more body heat has the potential to help heat the room. You will also need fewer resources to heat a smaller room.
- Enclosed – the room should be closed off on all sides. If there is a stairwell, it should be sealed off when used as an Emergency Off Grid Room.
- Windows – consider choosing a room in your home with the fewest & smallest windows. Windows can let out a significant amount of heat!
- Comfortable – yes, you want a small room, but you also want a room where your family will be comfortable. Nights are usually the coolest, so I want an area where my family and I can gather for the evening and enjoy each other's company in warmth.
- Backup light source- you will want a light that's not connected to city power. Lanterns and battery powered light bulbs work best for multiple people.
- Heat source

2.3.3 Energy & Fuel Checklist

Alternative Energy Checklist	Location
○	
○	
○	
○	
○	
○	
○	
○	
○	
○	
○	

Fuel Checklist	Location
○	
○	
○	
○	
○	
○	
○	
○	
○	
○	
○	
○	

Having off-grid options are helpful in a power outage. Below list 3 off-grid methods you want in your emergency supplies:

Alternative Energy

○ 1st _____

○ 2nd _____

○ 3rd _____

Alternative energy ideas: solar panels, wind turbine, water wheel, a generator (gas, solar, inverter).

Fuel supply ideas: kerosene, propane, charcoal briquette, gasoline cans, siphon, matches, lighters.

Off-grid Room

List the area in your home that would make the best gathering place to conserve resources.

○ _____

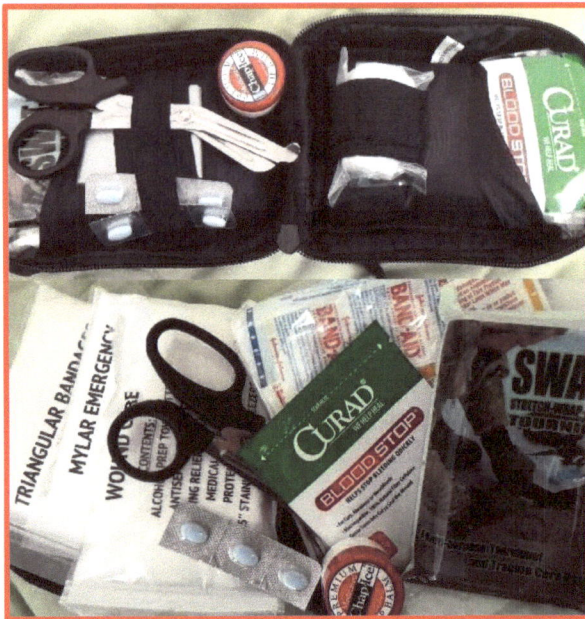

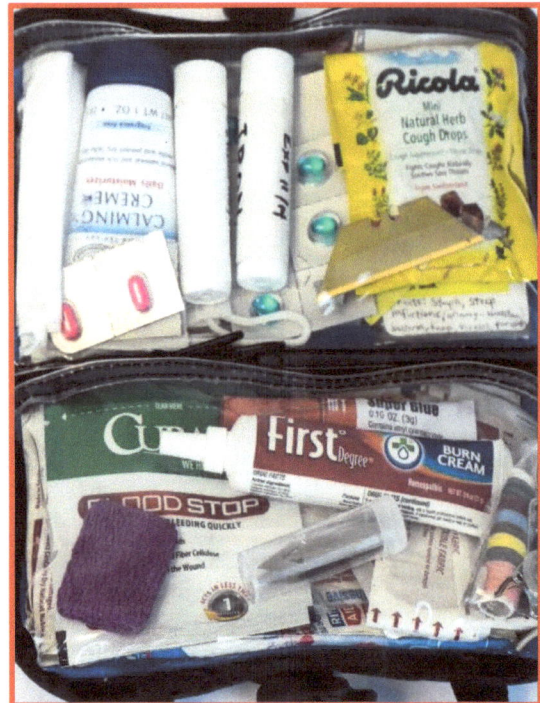

Keeping wounds clean and covered is an essential part of surviving an emergency. When not treated, an infected wound can be life-threatening. Trained medical care may not be available, so prevention is very important. Having a basic first aid kit could save your life and can help you stay healthy.

Start with a basic store bought kit and add some important items like blood clot powder, burn cream and antibiotics. After taking the kit on several adventures. I felt like my kit was missing items that would have been helpful like moleskin, anti-diarrhea pills, and a razor blade. First aid kits can be a pricey prep if you buy it all at once. However, you can start with a basic kit and slowly add to it each month. Some of the pricier items are blood clot powder, burn cream, and good tweezers.

Above are pictures of two bug out first aid kits. They serve me well on the many road trips, hiking adventures, and trips to the gun range. I get dehydrated very quickly; my skin starts to crack and bleed, so my kit has lotion, lip balm, and hydration powder that aren't found in most people's first aid kit. Everyone's first aid kit should be a little different; it should be tailored to fit the needs of your family.

○ Acetaminophen	○ Antacid
○ Antibiotic ointment	○ Antibiotics
○ Anti-constipation capsules	○ Anti-diarrhea pills
○ Anti-fungal ointment	○ Antihistamine (allergy)
○ Anti-inflammatory	○ Antiseptic
○ Blood clot powder	○ Band aids
○ Blood pressure kit	○ Burn cream
○ Charcoal (poison absorber)	○ Cough drops
○ Dental emergency kit	○ Eye drops
○ First aid guide booklet	○ Gauze pads
○ Hemorrhoid cream	○ Instant cold packs
○ Iodine	○ Medical tape
○ Medical scissors	○ Moleskin
○ Petroleum Jelly	○ Prescription medication
○ Rash cream	○ Razors
○ Salt (saline solution)	○ Scalpel
○ Sewing kit	○ Snake bite kit
○ Splint	○ Super glue
○ Support braces (knee, wrist)	○ Surgical gloves
○ Surgical masks	○ Surgical tape
○ Thermometer (non-digital)	○ Tourniquet
○ Tweezers	○ Vitamins
○	○
○	○
○	○
○	○
○	○

First Aid

There are many places where it may be useful to have a first aid kit. I have a large kit that is kept with my emergency supplies, also I have several smaller kits. Here are some places smaller kits are stored: bathrooms, cars, bug out bags, gun range bag, purse, and work.

Below list the three locations where you'll keep your largest first aid kits.

First Aid Kit Locations:

○   1st _____

○   2nd _____

○   3rd _____

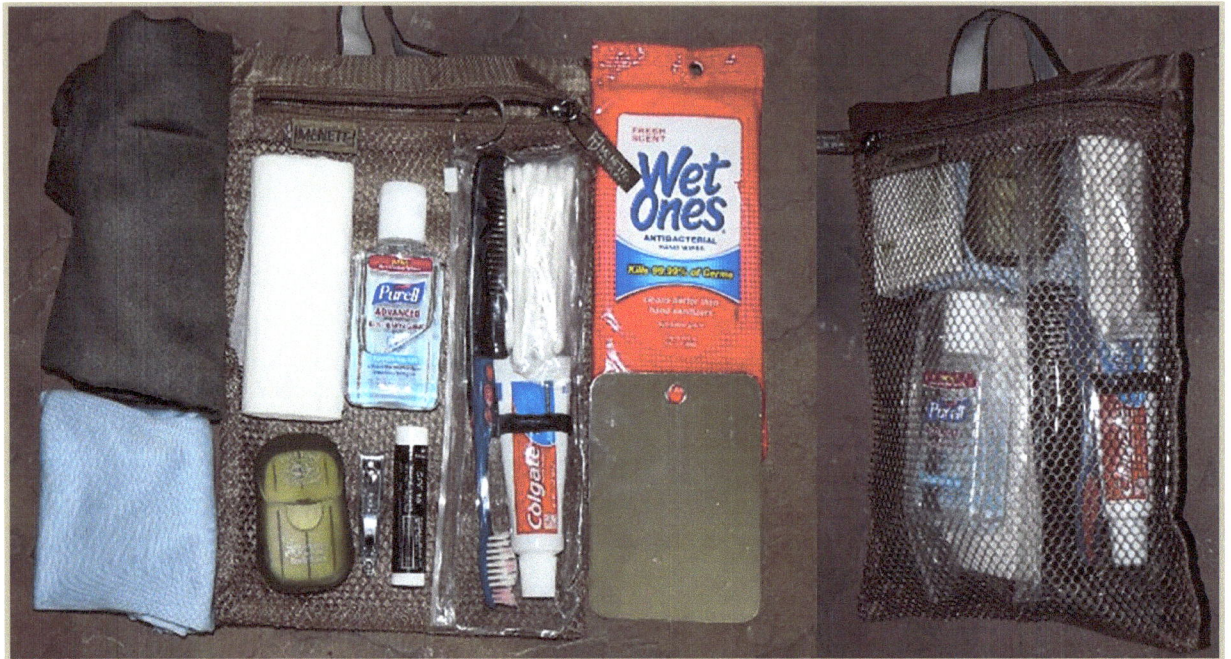

2.5 HYGIENE SUPPLIES CHECKLIST	LOCATION
○ Baby wipes	
○ Barber comb & scissors	
○ Chap-stick	
○ Cotton swabs	
○ Dental kit	
○ Deodorant	
○ Diapers	
○ Disinfectant Wipes	
○ Hair brush, comb, & hair-ties	
○ Hair shampoo & conditioner	
○ Hand sanitizer	
○ Lime oil (removes grease & sap)	
○ Lotion	
○ Nail clippers	
○ Sanitary pads (reusable)	
○ Soap – antibacterial hand soap	
○ Soap – bar soap/bath wash	
○ Soap – laundry detergent	
○ Straight razor & sharpener	
○ Toilet Paper	
○ Toothbrushes	
○ Toothpaste	
○ Tweezers	
○	
○	
○	
○	

Hygiene

Hygiene supplies are an essential part of good health and comfortable living. However, hygienic care is often the overlooked prep.

Having off-grid options are helpful in a power outage. Below list off-grid methods for hygiene you want in your emergency supplies:

Off-Grid Hygiene:

○ *Off-grid toilet*

○ *Washbasin*

○ *Camping shower*

Get recipes for:

○ *Homemade toothpaste*

○ *Homemade soap*

Grow:

○ *Loofa Sponges*

○ *Mint (for toothpaste & soap)*

COMMUNICATION

In an emergency, the first resource that people want is a way to send and receive information. Being connected plays a vital role in our sense of safety and well-being. Create a plan to connect with your loved ones in a crisis. Below are some ideas to help you create an emergency communication and evacuation plan for your family.

○ A code word to authenticate a message came from a family member

○ A warning word that lets your family know you are in a bad situation

○ Emergency contact list (see page 23)

○ Emergency meet-up locations (see page 23)

○ Photos of your family or emergency group

○ A map of alternate routes out of your area

○ Create an emergency contact group in your cell phone

○ Join or start a local Facebook group

2.6	COMMUNICATION SUPPLIES	LOCATION
○		
○		
○		
○		
○		
○		
○		
○		
○		
○		
○		
○		
○		

Having a secondary method to get local news updates and communicate with family, friends, and neighbors can be vital in a crisis. Below list 3 methods to receive news you want in your supplies:

Communication Source:

○ 1st _____

○ 2nd _____

○ 3rd _____

Communication Ideas:

AM/FM radio, NOAA radio, shortwave radio, ham radio, satellite phone, CB radio, and long range walkie talkies.

Additional Communication Supply Ideas:

Battery bank, cheat-sheet for Morse Code, cheat-sheet for Phonetic Alphabet, faraday cage, flares, postage stamps, GPS, long-range antennas, maps, atlas, compass, whistle.

A little before 5 pm, my computer monitor along with all the other electronics in my home went dark. I plugged my dying cell phone into a battery bank then used it to search the web for news. An explosion at a substation power plant caused a massive power outage. Next, I texted my husband and nearby family members. They were all safe and appreciated the news. Then I posted the story on a local Facebook group. The group was a valuable resource. We quickly discovered how far the power outage extended based on the updates everyone was getting from their family and friends. Getting news came faster from networking than it did from the power company. I did not have to wait and worry about what was happening in the world. With some basic preps, I could quickly determine the problem and connect with loved ones.

2.7 EMERGENCY CONTACT LIST

Emergency Meet-Up Locations

Inside City Limits: (name & address)
1. _____
2. _____

Outside City Limits:
_____

Outside State Limits
_____

Name: _____
1st Phone #: _____
2nd Phone #: _____
1st Address: _____
2nd Address: _____
Email: _____
Notes: _____

Name: _____
1st Phone #: _____
2nd Phone #: _____
1st Address: _____
2nd Address: _____
Email: _____
Notes: _____

Name: _____
1st Phone #: _____
2nd Phone #: _____
1st Address: _____
2nd Address: _____
Email: _____
Notes: _____

Name: _____
1st Phone #: _____
2nd Phone #: _____
1st Address: _____
2nd Address: _____
Email: _____
Notes: _____

Name: _____
1st Phone #: _____
2nd Phone #: _____
1st Address: _____
2nd Address: _____
Email: _____
Notes: _____

Name: _____
1st Phone #: _____
2nd Phone #: _____
1st Address: _____
2nd Address: _____
Email: _____
Notes: _____

Name: _____
1st Phone #: _____
2nd Phone #: _____
1st Address: _____
2nd Address: _____
Email: _____
Notes: _____

2.8 FAMILY IDENTIFICATION

During an evacuation, family members can be separated and take days or weeks to locate. Having a photo can assist you in a search to locate a lost family member.

Name: _____   Name: _____   Name: _____

DOB: _____   DOB: _____   DOB: _____

Name: _____   Name: _____   Name: _____

DOB: _____   DOB: _____   DOB: _____

[Family Photo Here]

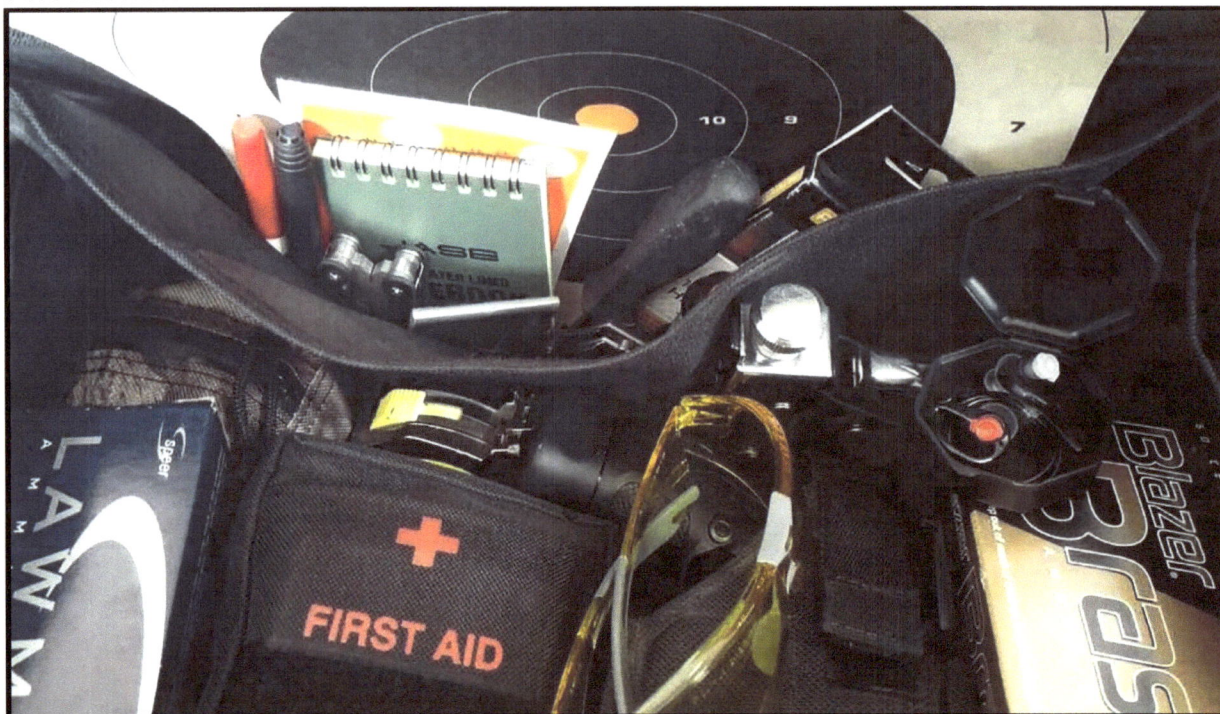

My husband may never forgive me for telling this story, but it demonstrates an important lesson. We planned a trip to go hiking through Kings Canyon, one of California's National Parks. Being the Prepper that I am, I read up on the local animal life and what to do if we were to have a dangerous animal encounter. So, there we were hiking through the forest and suddenly, a bear appears and is coming toward us. On the hike, I had picked up a fist sized rock and held my pepper spray in the other hand. Holding my ground, I started shouting and threw the rock in the bear's general direction. My tough guy husband (whom I trust with my life and who has jumped to my rescue many times when confronting the dogs on our regular walking path) who was leading the way somehow ended up behind me. He was unconsciously using me as a human shield because he was faced with something unexpected. I am happy to report that the bear moved on and I was able to resuscitate my husband. Being prepared lessened the shock of oncoming danger and I could act quickly which improved our chances of safety.

2.9 PROTECTION & HUNTING CHECKLIST	LOCATION
○	
○	
○	
○	
○	
○	
○	
○	
○	
○	
○	
○	
○	
○	
○	
○	
○	
○	
○	
○	
○	

Below list 3 methods of protection you want in your emergency supplies:

Protection

○ 1st _____

○ 2nd _____

○ 3rd _____

Protection ideas: *bat, dog, handgun, home security system, pepper spray, rifle, shot gun.*

Additional Protection & Hunting Supply Ideas:

Ammo, baton, dust mask, carbon monoxide detector, cross bow, extra gun magazines, fire extinguishers, gas mask, gun cleaning kit, hunting bow, knife, machete, mosquito net, motion detector perimeter lights, smoke detectors, snare kit, rodent traps, safe, spare gun parts.

2.10 FINANCIAL CHECKLIST

Level One – Set Financial Goals
○ Use a debt elimination plan
○ Save at least 10% of your paycheck
○ Live within a budget
○ Use cash instead of debit/credit cards
○ Create a two-week plan for home cooked meals
○ Have a two-week supply of food storage
○ Donate 10% of your earning to a charitable cause

Level Two – Create A Shelter
○ $1100 emergency fund in your savings account
○ Have a month supply of food storage
○ No credit card debt, auto loans, student loans
○ Auto insurance
○ Health insurance
○ Home/Renter insurance
○ Life insurance
○ Will/Life estate

Level Three – Build a Foundation by Diversifying Assets
○ 6 months' worth of expense in your savings account
○ 6 months of food storage and emergency supplies
○ College degree, professional license, or trade
○ Food self-reliance (plant a garden & raise chickens)
○ Own your home (mortgage-free)
○ Retirement plan
○ Liability insurance
○ Disability insurance

Level Four – Plan for Growth & Economic Changes
○ 12 months' worth of expense in your saving account
○ 12 months of food storage and emergency supplies
○ Develop a skill that'll be needed during economic hardship
○ Renewable commodity. Cultivate a commodity that will provide resources to barter with (beehive: honey & wax)
○ Residual income (rental property, business owner, write a book, blog)
○ Renewable energy for your home. Work towards living off the grid and becoming self-reliant.

Bugout Bag

There are many reasons for an evacuation kit: flooding, fire, famine, and terrorism are the most common in the news. Stories of evacuees have caught my attention over the years. Some of the items I remember they wish they had grabbed are medication, good shoes, clothes, toiletries, laptops, photos, identification, and keepsakes.

The idea behind the bugout bag is to leave a situation quickly with four days of essential survival supplies and personal items you may need or want.

For bugout bag food ideas visit:

http://www.prepperssurvive.com/bug-bag-food-ideas/

2.11 BUGOUT BAG CHECKLIST	LOCATION
○	
○	
○	
○	
○	
○	
○	
○	
○	
○	
○	
○	
○	
○	
○	
○	

Bug Out Bag Supply Ideas

FOOD & WATER
- ○ Food rations for four days   ○ Fishing kit
- ○ 32 oz water bottle (It's recommended to drink 8 oz, 8x a day = 64oz.)
- ○ Water purification tablets
- ○ Camping cook set, utensil, scrubbing pad

LIGHT & WARMTH
- ○ Flashlight with extra batteries and/or solar/hand crank light
- ○ Glow sticks   ○ Candles   ○ Flares
- ○ Matches, lighter, and/or magnifying glass (another method to start fires)
- ○ Hand or foot warmers
- ○ Emergency blanket and/or light weight blanket
- ○ Sleeping bag
- ○ Tent

CLOTHING
- ○ Extra clothing (shirt, pants, thermals, underwear, socks, shoes, boots)
- ○ Beanie, baseball cap, & handkerchief
- ○ Gloves
- ○ Belt
- ○ Poncho

FIRSTAID
○ Variety of bandages	○ Antibiotic ointment	○ Surgical gloves
○ Medication/vitamins	○ Tweezers	○ Small sewing kit
○ Eye drops	○ Moleskin	○ Crazy glue
○ Pain reliever	○ Headache medicine	○ Allergy medicine

TOILETRIES
○ Toothbrush	○ Toothpaste	○ Cotton swabs
○ Brush or comb	○ Lotion	○ Hair ties
○ Toilet paper	○ Feminine hygiene	○ Hand shovel
○ Hand sanitizer	○ Small bar of soap	○ Washcloth

COMMUNICATION
○ Radio & a list of radio stations	○ Notepad & pencil	○ Calling card
○ Stamps & postcards	○ Battery charger	○ Prepaid phone
○ Whistle		

MISCELLANEOUS
○ Duct tape	○ Black garbage bags	○ Multitool
○ Map	○ Compass	○ Scriptures
○ Pocket knife/Razor blade	○ Pepper spray	○ Rope

- ○ Stress relievers-a favorite book, puzzles, games, or toys
- ○ An inventory list of everything in your emergency kit

DOCUMENTS - Carry Copies Of:
○ Picture of family members	○ Licenses & certifications (drivers, medical)
○ Contact info of family & friends	○ Copies of prescription medications
○ Other copies of docs that have value to you	

3 HOW TO USE THE PREPPER CALENDAR

Ever wondered what the preparedness community is up to each month? We not only have the National Preparedness month in September, but there are eleven other national observance months that make up the 12-month prepper calendar. Here are several uses for this prepper calendar:

- **Save money on emergency preparedness supplies** – In the month of April, National Garden Month, there are great sale prices on garden supply preps. In the month of June, National Great Outdoors Month, you can save on camping essentials or items for a bug out bag.

- **Explore new preparedness ideas** – October is Energy Awareness Month. There are new articles, product launches, and resources that become available on the latest renewable, self-sufficient energy sources.

- **Connect with like-minded individuals** – It is common among preppers to feel isolated in their belief of "Being Prepared." You may be the only Prepper within your family, friends, or even neighborhood. The prepper calendar can help you locate trade shows, classes, and events where you can connect with our ever-growing prepper community. Just do an internet search of the national observation month and your state or community. Example: "Ham Radio Field Day Idaho."

- **Awareness** – I am a big believer in spreading preparedness awareness. Community activities such as fairs, trade-shows, and expos are great resources in spreading community preparedness awareness. By supporting these events, more events and resources will become available which is one of the simplest ways to grow the number of Preppers in your community.

Beginning Preppers List – It is helpful to have a guide when taking on a large project. Gathering all the preparedness supplies you need can be simple. The prepper calendar was designed to provide a simplified supply gathering plan. Each month provides a category to focus on and work towards gathering supplies.

5 EXTRA CHECKLIST

Extra checklist ideas: tools, gardening, professional trade, cooking ingredients, spices.

○	
○	
○	
○	
○	
○	
○	
○	
○	
○	
○	
○	
○	
○	
○	
○	
○	
○	
○	
○	
○	
○	
○	
○	
○	

○	
○	
○	
○	
○	
○	
○	
○	
○	
○	
○	
○	
○	
○	
○	
○	
○	
○	
○	
○	
○	
○	
○	
○	
○	
○	

○	
○	
○	
○	
○	
○	
○	
○	
○	
○	
○	
○	
○	
○	
○	
○	
○	
○	
○	
○	
○	
○	
○	
○	
○	

○	
○	
○	
○	
○	
○	
○	
○	
○	
○	
○	
○	
○	
○	
○	
○	
○	
○	
○	
○	
○	
○	
○	
○	
○	
○	

○	
○	
○	
○	
○	
○	
○	
○	
○	
○	
○	
○	
○	
○	
○	
○	
○	
○	
○	
○	
○	
○	
○	
○	
○	
○	

○	
○	
○	
○	
○	
○	
○	
○	
○	
○	
○	
○	
○	
○	
○	
○	
○	
○	
○	
○	
○	
○	
○	
○	
○	

6 THANK YOU

Thank you for purchasing the Prepper Supplies Checklist. Purchasing preparedness books, like this one, is a great way to support the efforts of the prepper community in spreading the message of emergency preparedness.

If you found this book helpful, please take a minute to write a review of this book on Amazon.

Most of the content contained in this book was originally posted on PreppersSurvive.com throughout many posts. On the website, there is a search bar located at the top right (under the social media icons). I invite you to use it if you would like more information on a topic.

My email address is contact@preppersurvive.com and I would love to hear from you when you have ideas or questions about this book. Your feedback is appreciated and helps me to provide better material in future publications.

Sincerely,

Nettie

www.ingramcontent.com/pod-product-compliance
Lightning Source LLC
Chambersburg PA
CBHW060900270326
41935CB00004B/54

9 780692 886649